BUSH AND HIGH COUNTRY BIRDS OF NEW ZEALAND

This book is the second in a new series designed to help bird watchers identify common or especially interesting New Zealand birds. It includes 28 birds of the New Zealand bush and high country, each illustrated in full colour. Sketches also show the birds in action poses, and species which can be confused are grouped together. A further advantage of this work is the greater size of the painted specimens, compared with those commonly shown in bird guides.

The text is deliberately concise, consisting mainly of features than cannot be easily illustrated, and some useful facts about behaviour and relationships — species, genus, family.

Books by Elaine Power

Small Birds of the New Zealand Bush (Collins)
Waders in New Zealand (Collins)
New Zealand Water Birds (Collins)
Seabirds of New Zealand (Collins)
Elaine Power's Living Garden (Hodder)
Countryside and Garden Birds of New Zealand (Bateman)

Books illustrated by Elaine Power

Tat, by Neil McNaughton (Collins)
The Horse in New Zealand, by Len McClelland (Collins)
Wild Manes in the Afternoon, by Mary Cox (Collins)
The New Guide to the Birds of New Zealand, by Falla *et al.* (Collins)
The Herb Garden Displayed, by Gillian Painter (Hodder)
A Touch of Nature, by Muriel Fisher (Collins)
Old Fashioned and Unusual Herbs, by Gillian Painter (Hodder)
Our Trees, by Frank Newhook (Bateman)
Call of the Kotuku, by Janet Redhead (Hodder)
The Pohutukawa Tree, by Ron Bacon (School Pubs.)

BUSH AND HIGH COUNTRY BIRDS
OF NEW ZEALAND

Elaine Power

DAVID BATEMAN
AUCKLAND

About the Artist

Elaine Power was born in Auckland in 1931, educated at Diocesan High School for Girls in Auckland and spent a year at the Elam School of Fine Arts. Was a librarian at the Remuera Library for five years. After a year as a doctor's receptionist spent the years before marriage, with the mapping department of the Automobile Association. Married Gerald Aldworth Power. When their third daughter was three, started painting again and submitted designs to the Crown Lynn Pottery Design competition, in which she was highly commended. In 1968 her first book was commissioned; since then six of her own books have been published and she has illustrated 10 others.

© Elaine Power 1988

First published in 1988
by David Bateman Ltd,
'Golden Heights', 32–34 View Road, Glenfield,
Auckland, New Zealand

Typeset by Typocrafters Ltd
Printed by Colorcraft Ltd, Hong Kong

ISBN 0-908610-88-2

Contents

Introduction

Centuries ago New Zealand was a land of birds and Joseph Banks, botanist with Captain Cook, aptly described the dawn chorus as "the most melodious wild music I have ever heard. The forest rang with the Bell like notes, chortles and shrieks as the large number of birds filled the air with song."

The Maori had a great respect for the birds of the forest and the feathers were highly valued for hair adornment and for clothing. Kiwi feathers were carefully woven into a base of flax fibre to make the prized kiwi cloaks, while the bright feathers of the kaka, stitchbird, kakapo and pigeon were woven into the borders of other garments. Huia tail feathers were treasured for hair adornment and warriors would wear twelve feathers in their hair to represent war plumes (marereko). These were kept in beautifully carved boxes called waka huia. The Maori relied on birds for food and tui, kaka, parakeets and pigeons were patiently snared, while weka were both snared and hunted with the help of dogs.

All the moas as well as several birds of prey and a number of endemic ducks, swan and geese died out before the arrival of Europeans. With European settlement cities, pastureland, crops and plantations replaced those large forested areas and with the loss of habitat many of the bird species also disappeared. The laughing owl, huia and piopio (New Zealand thrush) are now extinct. Many European birds were introduced by settlers and several Australian birds have found their own way to New Zealand and become established here.

Today all native birds are protected, and through the establishment of national parks, reserves, island sanctuaries, and increased interest in conservation, the numbers of birds may grow until once again we call New Zealand a land of birds.

The birds in this book have been placed in family groups but are not in any special order. Where there is a difference in plumage between male and female, both are illustrated, while in cases where sexes are similar only one bird is depicted.

Maori names

Hiti	Stitchbird
Kaka	
Kakariki	Red-crowned *or* yellow-crowned parakeet
Karearea	Falcon
Kawekawea	Long-tailed cuckoo
Kea	
Kereru	Pigeon
Kiwi	
Koekoea	Long-tailed cuckoo
Kohoperoa	Long-tailed cuckoo
Kokako	
Korimako	Bellbird
Kotihe	Stitchbird
Kuku	Pigeon
Kukupa	Pigeon
Makomako	Bellbird
Miromiro	Tomtit
Mohua	Yellowhead
Ngirungiru	Tomtit
Pipipi	Brown creeper
Pipiwharauroa	Shining cuckoo
Piwakawaka	Fantail
Popokatea	Whitehead
Riroriro	Grey warbler
Ruru	Morepork
Tauhou	Silvereye
Tieke	Saddleback
Tihi	Stitchbird
Tiora	Stitchbird
Titipounamu	Rifleman
Toutouwai	Robin
Weka	

The birds seen in New Zealand can be categorised as follows:

Endemic   Found and breeding in New Zealand only.

Native or indigenous Found and breeding in New Zealand, but also found in other countries.

Introduced   Released into New Zealand by man.

♂ male   ♀ female

Acknowledgements

Thanks to R. B. Sibson and Peter Gaze for checking illustrations and text respectively.

Books used for reference

The New Guide to the Birds of New Zealand, R. A. Falla *et al.*, 1979, Collins.

New Zealand Birds, W. R. B. Oliver, 1974, A. H. & A. W. Reed.

Birds of New Zealand & Outlying Islands, M. F. Soper, 1984, Whitcoulls.

Annotated Checklist of the Birds of New Zealand, F. C. Kinsky *et al.*, 1970, A. H. & A. W. Reed. *Amendments and additions*, 1980.

Birds of the World, O. L. Austin, 1961, Paul Hamlyn.

Living Birds of the World, E. T. Gilliard, 1959, Hamish Hamilton.

Reader's Digest Complete Book of New Zealand Birds, 1985, Reed Methuen.

KIWIS:
Family Apterygidae

Brown kiwi — *Apteryx australis.* 50 cm.
Little spotted kiwi — *Apteryx owenii.* 40 cm.
Great spotted kiwi — *Apteryx haastii.* 50 cm.

New Zealand's famous kiwis are adapted for a nocturnal life on the forest floor. They all have long, sensitive bills with nostrils at the tip, for probing under the leaf litter in search of food. Kiwis have only remnants of wings, and like the moas to which they are related, lack a keel on the breastbone for attachment of flight muscles. Though kiwis have weak eyesight, long bristles around their mouths help them feel their way through the undergrowth at night. All three species have similar habits and are distinguished by their sizes, colours and patterns, as the names imply. The brown kiwi occurs widely throughout the North, South and Stewart Islands, while both the spotted kiwis are confined to western districts of the South Island. Kiwis lay usually one very large egg in a burrow or hollow log, and only the male incubates.

ear

Kiwi

running

Kiwi digging in leaf litter.

Little Spotted Kiwi.

feather.

NORTH ISLAND BROWN KIWI

NEW ZEALAND PIGEON

PIGEONS, DOVES:
Family Columbidae

Pigeons and doves are found throughout the world in many different environments from tropical rain forests to harsh deserts, wherever there is a supply of fruits, berries and seeds. Because of their adaptability, some species have become domesticated and are found in many cities. Even though they vary in size from large, stout birds with short tails to small, delicate species with long tails, they all have small heads. Their colouring can vary from soft, subtle shades to bright oranges, yellows, greens and blues. Unlike other birds, pigeons and doves are able to swallow without tilting their heads back, and do not need to tilt their heads to drink. They feed their chicks on ''pigeon milk'', a white, protein-rich substance which is regurgitated from the crop.

New Zealand pigeon — *Hemiphaga novaeseelandiae.* 50 cm.

The endemic New Zealand pigeon belongs to a subfamily of the fruit pigeons that are found around the south Pacific, Asia, Malaysia and Africa. Although their natural habitat is the forest, they will venture into gardens and parks in search of the fruits and leaves of certain ornamental trees and shrubs. Because they swallow fruit whole they play a great part in the dispersal of seed and regeneration of forests. Their flight is normally strong and direct, with a distinct swishing sound, but when breeding they will perform an amazing aerial display of swooping skywards, stalling, then dropping downwards. As with other pigeons, the nests are flimsy constructions in small branches of trees, upon which a single white egg is laid.

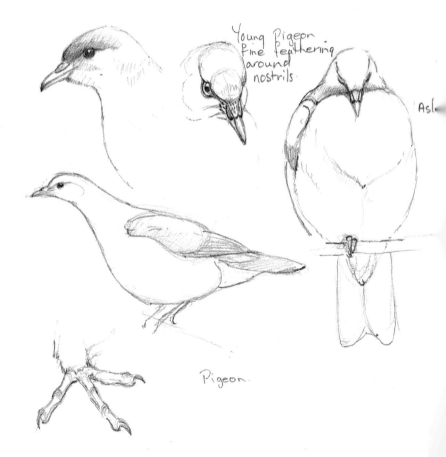

Young Pigeon
Fine feathering
around
nostrils.

Asl.

Pigeon.

KAKAS, KEAS:
Family Nestoridae

The two subspecies of kaka and the kea make up this endemic family of parrots. Both are similar in shape and size, compact with broad tails and have strong, long, downward-curving bills. While the kakas are birds of the forest, keas live in the valleys and mountains of the high country.

Kea — *Nestor notabilis*. 46 cm.

Kea are similar in size to kaka with strong, curved bills, the female's bill being slightly longer and more slender than that of the male. They are extremely cheeky and inquisitive and have great pleasure examining anyone or anything that ventures into their territory. When in flight their distinct call of "ke, aa" resounds across the valleys. The kea normally feeds on roots, shoots, berries and insects but will readily feed on nectar or even carrion when available. During the breeding season most males will have one mate but some are polygamous. Their nests are hidden in holes in the ground, under logs and in cavities among boulders. The kea lays two to four white eggs which are incubated mostly by the female.

Young Kea.
Yellow eye lids
+ cere.

Pigeon toed

KEA

♂

♀

KAKA (see p. 16)

LVEREYES:
mily Zosteropidae

ough very small, silvereyes are remarkable for the
y they have successfully colonised oceanic islands
probably as a result of being caught in storms.

vereye — *Zosterops lateralis*. 12 cm.

e silvereye was first recorded in New Zealand last
tury, but is now well established in a variety of
itats throughout the country. It feeds on nectar,
t, and a wide range of insects, spiders and cater-
rs. During spring, silvereyes build a delicate cup-
ped nest hanging loosely between branches. The
ch is usually three pale blue eggs and both sexes
bate.

SILVEREYES

Kaka — *Nestor meridionalis*. 45 cm.

There are two subspecies of kaka endemic to New Zealand. The South Island kaka is slightly brighter in colouring than the North Island kaka and is also a lighter grey on the crown. They are large, noisy birds whose natural habitat is the native bush where there are stands of large and old trees. In contrast to this, an occasional pair will venture into parks and gardens in the Auckland area when food is not so plentiful. Like some other species of parrot they will call to each other during the night.

Kaka feed on a variety of food including berries, nectar and even insects, which are sought by tearing at dead or living wood with the strong beak. They are very active early in the morning and late in the evening, when they may be seen in small flocks, but during the day are more solitary and much quieter. Kaka nest in holes in trees and the clutch usually contains two to four eggs.

Kaka

NEW ZEALAND PARAKEETS:
Family Platycercidae

This is a family found in Australasia and New Caledonia. There are two species endemic to New Zealand, the red-crowned and the yellow-crowned, while the smaller, rare orange-fronted parakeet is now thought to be a colour morph rather than a separate species. They are slender, long-tailed birds of bright colouring with stout, slightly curved bills. All are birds of forest areas and move from one tree to another with a direct, swift flight.

Red-crowned parakeet — *Cyanoramphus novaezelandiae.*
♂ 28 cm.   ♀ 25 cm.

Yellow-crowned parakeet — *Cyanoramphus auriceps.*
♂ 25 cm.   ♀ 23 cm.

Like the kaka, these slender, long-tailed parakeets are birds of the forest. The yellow-crowned parakeet is found in forested areas of the North and South Islands but the red-crowned is more abundant on offshore islands, particularly in the Hauraki Gulf. A wide variety of food is taken including seeds and berries, which are held in one foot while being eaten. Time is also spent on the ground scratching amongst dead leaves, looking for insects. Nests are built in holes in trees and the five to nine eggs are incubated by the female while the male brings her food. There are separate subspecies of red-crowned parakeet on the Kermadecs, Chathams, and Antipodes Islands.

Parakeet

RED-CROWNED PARAKEETS

♀

♂

YELLOW-CROWNED PARAKEETS

♂

♀

Juvenile

FALCONS:
Family Falconidae

This family consists of many species that vary in size from the tiny (15–16 cm) falconets of South America, Malaya and Africa to the large (61 cm) caracaras of the United States of America and South America. Other members of this family include the kestrels, sparrowhawks, peregrines and Gyr falcons. All have a sharp notch on the upper mandible, an adaptation for tearing at meat, and long pointed wings which enable them to move at a great speed.

New Zealand falcon — *Falco novaeseelandiae.* 45 cm.

New Zealand falcon — *Falco novaeseelandiae.* 45 cm.

These endemic birds of prey are found in forest areas and tussock land of the North, South and Stewart Islands. They are fearless, solitary hunters which will patiently wait on a perch until prey is sighted. After a chase, they go into a swift, slanting dive, grabbing the victim in their strong talons as they pass by. Most of their prey are introduced birds but locusts, beetles, skinks and the occasional rabbit are taken. New Zealand falcons vary in size from one area to another and the females are generally slightly larger than the males. Nests are usually on the ground, on a ledge or under a log, or sometimes on a platform of vegetation in a tree. Two to four eggs are laid and the females raise the chicks while the males bring food to the nest. New Zealand falcons are fully protected.

Falcon

Juvenile.

CUCKOOS:
Family Cuculidae

This family includes some parasitic species and some which build their own nests and raise their own young. Included among these are the cuckoos of Europe and Asia, the coucals of Africa and Australia, the anis of the American tropics and the roadrunners of the United States of America. In New Zealand the oriental cuckoo from northern Asia, the pallid, the fan-tailed and the channel-billed cuckoos of Australia have been recorded as rare stragglers; while the shining and long-tailed cuckoos are regular visitors each year, arriving in spring from their wintering islands in the Pacific.

Long-tailed cuckoo — *Eudynamys taitensis*. 40 cm.

In its forest habitat the long-tailed cuckoo can be very hard to see due to its colouration and the way it perches lengthwise on a branch. It is more often heard than seen and will gather in groups at the top of trees, from where the long, drawn-out screech can be heard. The long-tailed cuckoo is a parasite, laying single eggs in the nests of white-head, yellowhead and brown creeper, and relying on the foster-parents to raise the young. Because of their carnivorous habits, eating the eggs and young of other birds, they are often mobbed and driven off. They also feed on insects and lizards, and have been known to attack birds larger than themselves.

Long-tailed Cuckoo

Facing page:
Shining cuckoo — *Chrysococcyx lucie*
16 cm.

During August the shining cuckoo arr
after wintering in the Solomon Islands.
bird is more often heard than seen, bec:
of its cryptic colouration, and has a dist:
musical call that rises to a peak and then
away. They feed on insects. The shi
cuckoo lays a single egg in the nest of a
warbler but may visit several nests du
a season. As the young cuckoo grov
either pushes out or crushes the other
or chicks. Shining cuckoos frequent fo
scrub and gardens wherever foster pa:
can be found. They go back to the is!
in February and March.

LONG-TAILED CUC

SHINING CUCKOO

GREY WARBLER (see p. 24-25)

FLYCATCHERS, WARBLERS:
Family Muscicapidae

There are many different families of birds that catch insects in flight. The Muscicapidae or Old World flycatchers are found in Africa, Europe, Indonesia, Australia, New Zealand and the Pacific Islands. They are mainly birds of the forest but some species are quite tame and will venture into parks and gardens. They all have flattened bills with bristles around the base which help snare insects.

Members of the genera *Rhipidura* and *Petroica* are found in Australia, South Pacific Islands and New Zealand. In New Zealand there are three endemic species, the robin, the tomtit and the Chatham Islands black robin. The fantail is a native bird with separate subspecies in the North Island, South Island and Chatham Islands as well as Australia.

Grey warbler — *Gerygone igata*. 11 cm.

The grey warbler is one of the commonest and most vocal birds of the forest. It is always on the move and will hover in front of the leaves of shrubs, searching for insects. Being very adaptable, grey warblers even frequent gardens, where they are often seen in pairs. They build the most elaborately woven, enclosed nests from grasses, moss and spider webs, lined with feathers. The three to six pale eggs blotched with brown are incubated by the female only, but the young are fed by both parents. Grey warblers are used as foster parents by the shining cuckoo.

Grey Warbler

Grey warbl. chicks.

Whiteheads.

Juvenile Brown Creepers.

Whitehead — *Mohoua albicilla.* 15 cm.

Yellowhead — *Mohoua ochrocephala.* 15 cm.

Brown creeper — *Finschia novaeseelandiae.* 13 cm.

Whiteheads are found in forests and pine plantations of the North Island while yellowheads frequent the South Island forests. The brown creeper is found in forest, second-growth bush and scrub of the South and Stewart Islands. These very active, social birds spend most of their time searching for insects among the leaves and twigs of forest trees. Whiteheads and yellowheads will descend to the ground, then slowly work their way up the trunks of trees, using their tails for balance. Consequently the feathers become well-worn and look like spines. When searching the forks of branches yellowheads will use a foot for scratching out the dead leaves, in the same manner as a domestic fowl. Whiteheads and yellowheads are sometimes called "bush canaries" because of their pleasant song which is heard during the breeding season. Yellowheads have a much more powerful call.

(continued)

(Whitehead, yellowhead and brown creeper continued)
While whiteheads and brown creepers build their exquisite cup-shaped nests of bark, lichen and moss in small trees, shrubs and crevices of trees, yellowheads prefer a hole high in the canopy. Female whiteheads and yellowheads are browner on the head than the males while both sexes of the brown creeper are alike.

♂

YELLOWHEADS

♀

BROWN CREEPER

WHITEHEADS

South Island

Tomtit — *Petroica macrocephala.*
13 cm.

North Island

Robin — *Petroica australis.* 18 cm.

South Island

North Island

Robin — *Petroica australis*. 18 cm.

Robins are very inquisitive and will inspect any intruder on their territory, raising their frontal spots in display. They spend a lot of time on the ground searching for insects, worms and other invertebrates. The robin is most often found in native forest but in some areas is resident in pine plantations and second growth. Its nest resembles that of the tomtit and two or three eggs are laid, which are cream-coloured and spotted with purplish brown. There are three subspecies of robin: the North Island, South Island and Stewart Island. The Chatham Island robin is more distantly related.

Tomtit — *Petroica macrocephala*. 13 cm.

These inquisitive, friendly little tomtits are found in native forest, although the pied and yellow-breasted have adapted to living in pine plantations. Taking short flights, they hunt through the foliage of trees for insects, clinging sideways to trunks to scan the ground below for prey. They will put on an aggressive display when an intruder approaches. The nests, built by the females, are woven with cobwebs, moss and scraps of bark and lined with feathers. Nesting sites usually have overhead protection. While the females incubate the three to five cream-coloured, spotted eggs, they are fed by the males. There are five subspecies of tomtit: the pied, yellow-breasted, the Chatham Islands, the black tit of the Snares and the Auckland Islands tit.

Robin

Tomtit

Robin

Fantail — *Rhipidura fuliginosa.* 16 cm.

There are three subspecies of fantail: the North Island, South Island, and the Chatham Islands. Of all the New Zealand birds the fantails are the most endearing for their trust in people. Although they are forest birds they are quite at home in gardens and will catch flies in houses. With a darting flight they hunt insects, tails opening and closing as they move about. Their nests are delicate, cup-like constructions and usually have a tuft of material hanging from the bottom. Both parents build the nest and incubate the three or four cream-coloured, greyish-brown-spotted eggs.

Fantail

Bristles on face

Black phase

PIED FANTAIL

RIFLEMAN

NEW ZEALAND WRENS:
Family Acanthisittidae

The Stephens Island wren is now
extinct and the bush wren is rare,
leaving only the rock wren and rifleman as familiar members of this
endemic family. All New Zealand
wrens are similar in colouring but the
female rifleman has brown streaking.

Rifleman — *Acanthisitta chloris*. 8 cm.

Rifleman — *Acanthisitta chloris.* 8 cm.

The rifleman is the smallest bird in New Zealand and, being very active, is hard to see amongst the foliage of trees. With an incessant flicking of their wings they move up the trunks of trees searching every little crack in the bark for insects. They only fly short distances and move through the canopy of one tree to another. Riflemen build enclosed nests of grass and moss, with a side opening, in holes of trees or under peeling bark. They lay three or four white eggs, and both parents incubate. Sometimes the young of the first brood help to feed the second. Pairs may nest twice in a season.

Chick.

Juvenile Rifleman.

Rock Wren.

Rock wren — *Xenicus gilviventris*. 9.5 cm.

These small birds have incredibly large legs and feet, enabling them to cling to the rocky terrain which is their habitat. Weak flyers, they hop or flit from one rock to another. As they live in alpine areas of the South Island where it snows in winter, they rely on large boulders and rocky screes for protection. They have the unusual habit of bobbing up and down on one spot. Like the rifleman they build enclosed nests with a side entrance-hole, but the rock wren's nest is a bulky construction of roots, snowgrass and twigs hidden in the crevices of rocks. They lay two to five white eggs and both parents incubate.

ROCK WRENS

RAILS, COOTS, GALLINULES:
Family Rallidae

This is a diverse family of running, wading and swimming birds found in swamp and lake areas. They vary in size and shape from tiny crakes and rails to larger birds with frontal shields like the coots and gallinules. Two endemic New Zealand species that belong to this family are completely different to the other members: the large, brilliantly-coloured takahe and the compact, brown-plumaged weka. Both are flightless, even though they have rudimentary wings. The takahe differs from the other rails as its habitat is the tussock land of the high country. Wekas prefer scrub and farmland as well as the edges of forests.

Weka — *Gallirallus australis*. 50 cm.

Wekas are strong, fearless birds with an exceptional curiosity for anything that moves or is shiny. They have even been known to enter houses and steal small objects. Weka habitat varies from shorelines and swamp to scrub and forest. They are capable of moving swiftly over rough terrain. The diet varies from vegetation to birds' eggs and young, lizards, and even rabbits and mice which they run down. Well-concealed nests of grass lined with soft material are built on the ground under vegetation, rocky ledges, in burrows, and they have even been known to use outbuildings. Clutches of three to five eggs are laid and both parents incubate. The chicks are mobile just after hatching and will forage with the adults.

NORTH ISLAND WEKAS

(Weka continued)

There are four subspecies of the endemic weka: the North Island, the western, the buff and the Stewart Island. They are similar in size but vary in colouring from light buff to reddish brown and grey. The North Island wekas are common around Gisborne but have been released in other areas including Northland and Coromandel. South Island wekas are found in Southland, Fiordland, Westland, Nelson and Marlborough. The buff weka became extinct in its old habitat in the South Island but fortunately in the meantime had been successfully introduced to the Chatham Islands. It was then re-introduced to the Arthurs Pass National Park in 1962.

weka.

TUI, BELLBIRD & STITCHBIRD:
Family Meliphagidae (Honeyeaters)

Members of this predominantly Australasian and southwest Pacific family have curved, slender bills and specially adapted tongues for sipping nectar. Honeyeaters vary in size from the tiny 10-cm, brilliantly coloured birds of the Pacific Islands to the large 43-cm cape sugarbird of South Africa. As well as feeding on nectar they will take insects and fruits, thus becoming important pollinators of shrubs and trees; and by dispersing the seeds they play an important role in the regeneration of forests. In New Zealand all three species of honeyeater — tui, bellbird and stitchbird — are endemic. There are three subspecies of bellbird and two subspecies of tui.

Tui — *Prosthemadera novaeseelandiae*. 31 cm. 29 cm.

The tui is one of the finest songbirds of the New Zealand bush. Its song is loud and musical, interrupted with harsh coughs, clicks and rattles, and some notes are so high they are inaudible to human ears. When the birds fly their wingbeats are noisy and as they fly through the canopies of trees and shrubs they appear cumbersome. Tuis are strongly territorial and will aggressively chase any intruder. In the breeding season the males perform elaborate displays to attract females. Although nectar is their basic food, insects and fruits are also taken. Nests are bulky structures of sticks and twigs, built in the forks of outer branches of trees. The two to four eggs are white or pale pink with brown speckles and are incubated by the females.

Tui balancing in the wind.

ine line
white
eathers
gape

Juvenile Tui

Dark brown colouring. no white tufts under chin.

TUI

♂

♀

STITCHBIRD

♂

BELLBIRD

♂

♀

Stitchbird — *Notiomystis cincta.* ♂ 19 cm.   ♀ 18 cm.

The stitchbird is now found in abundance only on Little Barrier Island, but has been released on the Hen and Chickens, Cuvier and Kapiti Islands. Stitchbirds live in rain forest where there are tawa, tawhero, taraire, kohekohe and puriri trees. They build open nests of rootlets, sticks and fine materials in a hole in a tree, and the female incubates the four white eggs. The female stitchbird is brown, with white wing bars, and lacks the yellow breast-markings of the male.

Bellbird — *Anthornis melanura.* ♂ 20 cm.   ♀ 19 cm.

The beautiful song of the bellbird is made up of bell-like notes similar to those produced by the tui. Bellbirds build well-concealed nests of twigs and fern fibre, lined with soft material, in dense foliage. Three or four pink-white to deep pink eggs with pink blotches are incubated by the female, which tenaciously defends the nest and may even drop to the ground and flap away to distract the intruder. The bellbird is fairly common throughout forest areas, but, being rather shy, it is more often heard than seen.

Stitchbird ♂

Aggressive Bellbird

Bellbird bathing

Creamy-white band

Juvenile Bellbird

Stitchbird ♀

Juv Stitchbird

SADDLEBACK & KOKAKO:
Family Callaeidae (Wattlebirds)

Wattlebirds have limited powers of flight, as their wings are small and weak, so they rely more on their strong legs for movement through the trees. Both New Zealand species of wattlebird are forest dwellers and evolved in different ways so that they do not compete with each other. The saddleback's bill is narrow and pointed, adapted for tearing at bark and to extract wood-boring beetles and insects, while the kokako's bill is short and stout, for crushing fruit and berries. This is a very small family which once consisted of three species in New Zealand, but the huia has been extinct since about 1907 and both the saddleback and kokako are now limited in numbers and distribution.

Saddleback — *Philesturnus carunculatus*. 25 cm.

Since European settlement saddlebacks have declined in number and they are now found only in islands off the coast of New Zealand. There are two subspecies, which vary slightly in colouring. The North Island subspecies has a yellow band dividing the black and brown on the back.

(continued)

Saddleback displaying

Saddleback.

NORTH ISLAND SADDLEBACK

(Saddleback continued)
The South Island subspecies lacks the band and its juveniles are a uniform brown colour. Saddlebacks are very active and spend most of their time either foraging for food high in the canopy of trees or scratching among dead leaves on the ground. Favourite foods include wetas and grubs of tree-boring beetles, although they will eat berries in season. Saddlebacks are highly territorial and probably pair for life. Both sexes are similar in size and have small, orange wattles (fleshy lobes on the side of the face). They build cup-shaped nests in holes of trees or in dense vegetation where there is plenty of cover. The usual clutch is two pale brown, blotched eggs, which are incubated by the female.

SOUTH ISLAND SADDLEBACK (immature)

Kokako — *Callaeas cinerea.*
38 cm.

Kokako are long-legged birds of the dense virgin forest. As so much bush has now been cleared, the North Island subspecies now only exists in small populations in parts of the central North Island, Coromandel and Great Barrier Island. The South Island subspecies is near extinction but may

(continued)

KOKAKO

Kokako.

(Kokako continued)
still exist on Stewart Island. The two subspecies vary in the colouring of their wattles: blue in the North Island and orange with a blue base in the South Island subspecies. The birds characteristically move through the trees in long leaps and bounds using their wings for gliding short distances or flying to the ground. Their nests are untidy structures of small twigs, built high in the forked branches of trees. The female lays and incubates two or three eggs, similar in colouring to those of the saddleback. The young have small, pink wattles that change colour as they fledge.

MOREPORK:
Family Strigidae (Owls)

This family is nocturnal and members have large eyes and facial discs. Owls have large ears as they rely on hearing as well as sight to detect prey. For good vision they have the ability to turn their heads through an angle of 180°. Filaments on the edges of their wing feathers give the birds silent flight, and strong talons enable them to catch and hold their prey; fur and bones are regurgitated later in the form of pellets. Owls are found throughout the world in different environments from deserts, through the tropics, to the Arctic regions.

New Zealand has one native species, the morepork, plus the introduced little owl. The endemic laughing owl is now extinct.

Morepork — *Ninox novaeseelandiae.* 29 cm.

The morepork is common in New Zealand and has adapted to a wide range of habitats from forests to scrublands, farmlands and gardens. The familiar call, ''more-pork'' can be heard at night as they keep in contact with one another. The morepork is also found in Australia, where it is known as the Boobook Owl, and in New Guinea and at Norfolk Island. Mainly insectivorous, moreporks will also feed on lizards, mice and even small birds. Nesting takes place in hollow trees and only the females incubate. The clutch is usually two white eggs. Chicks remain in the nest for the comparatively long period of 5 weeks, guarded by the females, while the males bring food.

lick

Morepork

MOREPORKS

KAKAPO — *Strigops habroptilus.* 63 cm.
Family Cacatuidae

TAKAHE — *Notornis mantelli.* 63 cm
Family Rallidae

Kakapo, which are flightless ground parrots with facial feathering similar to owls, and the large, brilliantly coloured takahe, are both endemic to New Zealand. They are extremely rare so programmes have been set up to establish colonies on outlying islands and in captivity, to build up their numbers and so prevent extinction. They are birds of the high country, inhabiting tussock and scrub land in the valleys of Fiordland. A small population of kakapo also survives on Stewart Island. Although flightless, they both have small, weak wings. Kakapo have more developed wings than those of the takahe and use them for balance when moving down slopes or climbing. Both takahe and kakapo feed on tussock grasses, herbs and rhizomes of ferns. Kakapo nest in holes in the ground or at the base of trees, laying two or three white eggs. Takahe build their nests under the cover of tussock grasses, laying one or two cream, brown-blotched eggs.

Takahe

Kakapo